Countries We Come From

Thailand

by Chaya Glaser

Consultant: Marjorie Faulstich Orellana, PhD
Professor of Urban Schooling
University of California, Los Angeles

BEARPORT PUBLISHING

New York, New York

Credits

Cover, © TheJim999/Shutterstock and pat138241/iStock; TOC, © Butterfly Hunter/Shutterstock; 4, © PhilipYb Studio/Shutterstock; 5T, © Pixfly/iStock; 5B, © vectorx2263/Shutterstock; 7, © Kalamurzing/Shutterstock; 8, © Kim Petersen/Alamy; 9, © anekoho/Shutterstock; 9T, © Pisit Rapitpunt/Shutterstock; 10–11, © Prawat/Shutterstock; 10R, © hasachai/iStock; 11L, © kajornyot/iStock; 11R, © Boonchuay_Promjiam/iStock; 12T, © Ammar Mas-oo-di/AGE Fotostock; 12B, © Heinrich Damm/CC BY 4.0; 13, © Tanongsak Sangthong/Shutterstock; 14, © TWStock/Shutterstock; 15, © davidionut/iStock; 16L, © enviromantic/iStock; 16–17, © nimon_t/iStock; 18, © oneclearvision/iStock; 19, © silatip/iStock; 20T, © Phanuphong Thepnin/Dreamstime; 20B, © Toa555/Dreamstime; 21, © 1989studio/Shutterstock; 22, © cinoby/iStock; 23T, © WR36/Shutterstock; 23B, © rattanapatphoto/Shutterstock; 24–25, © LOVE_CHOTE/Shutterstock; 26L, © Benson HE/Shutterstock; 26–27, © Vassamon Anansukkasem/Shutterstock; 28, © topten22photo/iStock; 29, © topten22photo/Shutterstock; 30T, © ChewHow/Shutterstock and © Liumangtiger/Dreamstime; 30B, © Krzysztof Odziomek/Shutterstock; 31 (T to B), © Prapa Watchara/Shutterstock, © ake1150sb/iStock, © topten22photo/iStock, © Sura Nualpradid/Shutterstock, © FredFroese/iStock, and © puwanai/Shutterstock; 32, © happykanppy/Shutterstock.

Publisher: Kenn Goin
Senior Editor: Joyce Tavolacci
Creative Director: Spencer Brinker
Design: Debrah Kaiser
Photo Researcher: Thomas Persano

Library of Congress Cataloging-in-Publication Data

Names: Glaser, Chaya, author.
Title: Thailand / by Chaya Glaser.
Description: New York, New York : Bearport Publishing, 2019. | Series: Countries we come from | Includes bibliographical references and index.
Identifiers: LCCN 2018009260 (print) | LCCN 2018010083 (ebook) | ISBN 9781684027330 (Ebook) | ISBN 9781684026876 (library)
Subjects: LCSH: Thailand—Juvenile literature.
Classification: LCC DS563.5 (ebook) | LCC DS563.5 .G53 2019 (print) | DDC 959.3—dc23
LC record available at https://lccn.loc.gov/2018009260

For more information, write to Bearport Publishing Company, Inc., 45 West 21st Street, Suite 3B, New York, New York 10010. Printed in the United States of America.

10 9 8 7 6 5 4 3 2 1

Contents

This Is Thailand

Colorful

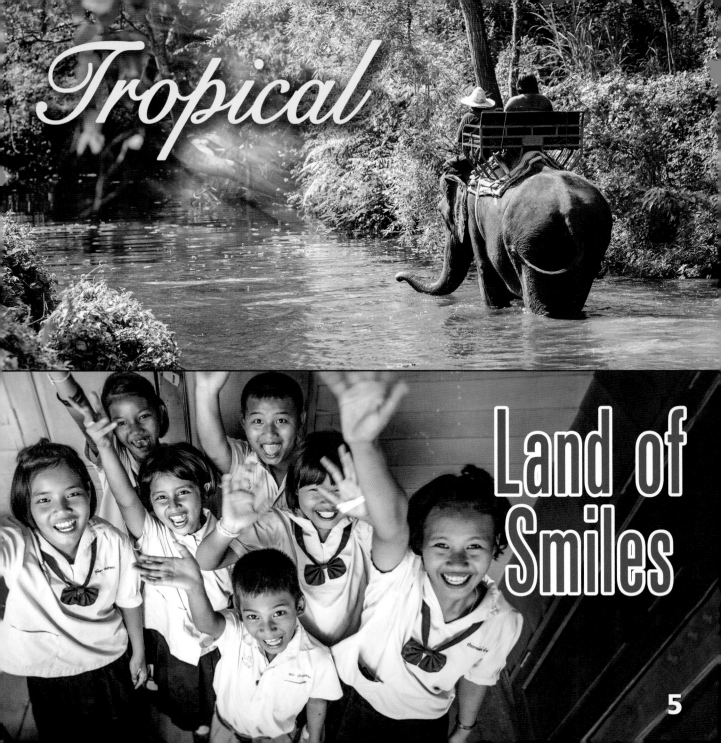

Tropical

Land of Smiles

Thailand is a country in Southeast Asia.

Over 68 million people live there.

Over 1,400 islands are part of Thailand!

The weather is warm and wet in Thailand.

During the rainy season, it pours almost every day!

The rainy season lasts from June to October.

The rain makes the country **lush** and green.

Thailand has deep forests, tall mountains, and sandy beaches.

Wild animals live in all of these places.

The elephant is a symbol of Thailand.

Look around!
You might spot elephants,
monkeys, and colorful birds.

People have been living in Thailand for thousands of years.

Early settlers left pottery and other **artifacts** behind.

Thailand was called Siam for hundreds of years.

The country has always been **independent**.

In fact, *Thailand* means "land of the free."

Thailand's **capital** is Bangkok. It's also the largest city in the country.

More than 9 million people live in Bangkok.

There are many beautiful buildings in Bangkok.

Temple Wat Arun

Where do Thai people shop?

Many visit floating markets!

They can buy almost anything there.

People sell fruit, fish, and flowers from their boats.

A floating market can have as many as 10,000 boats.

The main language in Thailand is Thai.

This is how you say *smile*:

Yim (YIM)

This is how you say *hello*:

Sawasdee (sah-WAH-dee)

When Thai people say hello or good-bye, they clasp their hands and bow. This is called a *wai*.

Thai food is fresh, spicy, and sweet.

People eat rice with most meals.

Over 5,000 types of rice come from Thailand!

mango

One Thai dessert is mango sticky rice. It's made with mango fruit, coconut, sugar, and rice.

21

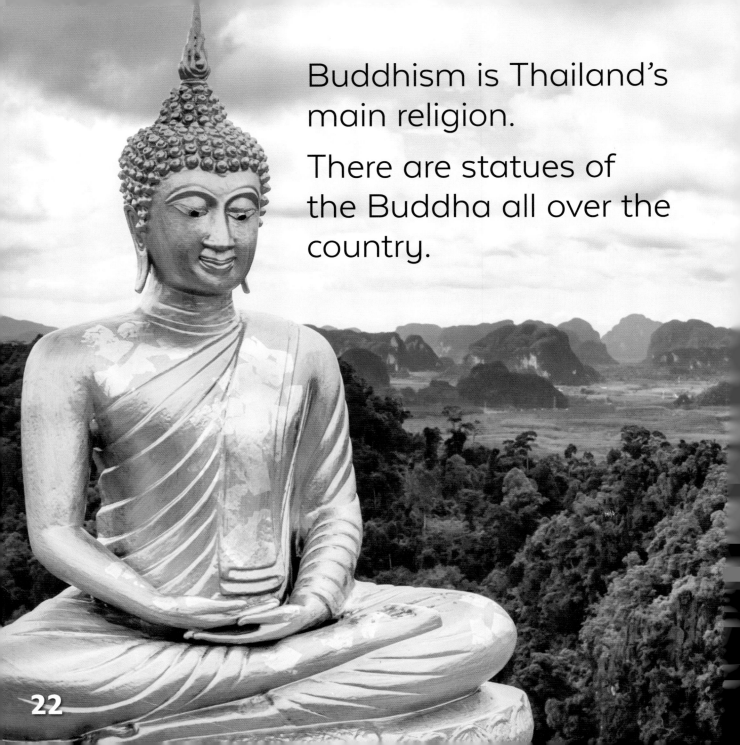

Buddhism is Thailand's main religion.

There are statues of the Buddha all over the country.

People **worship** in their homes and in temples.

The Buddha was an Indian prince. He left his home to learn about the world.

What sports do people in Thailand enjoy?

Muay Thai is like boxing and karate combined.

Fighters use their arms, legs, and feet!

Muay Thai is Thailand's most popular sport.

Lotus flowers fly through the air!

It's the Lotus Throwing **Festival**.

People try to toss the flowers into a boat for good luck.

lotus flower

The lotus festival is a big event in October. Thousands of people attend.

Once a year, there's a huge festival and feast.

The guests of honor aren't people, though.

They're monkeys!

The festival is called the Lopburi Monkey Buffet Festival. It takes place in November.

the monkeys of Lopburi having their feast

Fast Facts

Capital city: Bangkok

Population of Thailand: More than 68 million

Main language: Thai

Money: Thai Baht

Major religion: Buddhism

Neighboring countries: Myanmar (Burma), Laos, Malaysia, and Cambodia

Cool Fact: The whale shark is the largest fish in the world. It lives in the ocean waters around Thailand.

artifacts (ART-uh-fakts) objects of historical interest that were made by people

capital (KAP-uh-tuhl) a city where a country's government is based

festival (FESS-tuh-vuhl) a celebration or holiday

independent (in-di-PEN-duhnt) free of control from others

lush (LUHSH) rich, healthy, and thick

worship (WUR-ship) to adore and honor something

Index

Read More

Friedman, Mel. *Thailand (Enchantment of the World).* New York: Scholastic (2014).

Simmons, Walter. *Thailand (Blastoff! Readers: Exploring Countries).* New York: Scholastic (2010).

Learn More Online

To learn more about Thailand, visit
www.bearportpublishing.com/CountriesWeComeFrom

About the Author

Chaya Glaser loves going to other countries
and learning about different cultures. When she's
not traveling, she can be found playing
unusual musical instruments.